Four Cats Make One Pride

TEXT AND PHOTOGRAPHS BY

Elizabeth Kytle

SEVEN LOCKS PRESS

CABIN JOHN, MARYLAND

This book was set in Trump Medieval by Composition Systems, Inc., Arlington, Virginia.

Art direction by Richard Sisk, from an original design by Marilyn Housell. Production Assistance by Jeffrey J. Price, The Associates, Inc., Arlington, Virginia.

Printing by Prince Lithograph Company, Inc., Fairfax, Virginia.

Most of the color photographs were taken on Kodacolor II with an Olympus 35E C2. Black-and-white conversion by Image, Inc., of Washington, D.C.

Photographs on pages 44, 91, and 95 by Calvin Kytle.

The lines on page 7 are from *Old Possum's Book of Practical Cats*, copyright 1939 by T. S. Eliot. Harcourt, Brace and Company, Inc.

Library of Congress Cataloging in Publication Data

Kytle, Elizabeth Larisey.
   Four cats make one pride.

   1. Cats—Legends and stories. 2. Kytle, Elizabeth Larisey. I. Title
SF445.5.K9   818'.54'07   78-16603
ISBN 0-932020-00-3

SEVEN LOCKS PRESS
P.O. Box 72, 6600 81st Street,
Cabin John, Maryland 20731

Contents

Author's note

Although **Four Cats Make One Pride** is obviously a personal chronicle and in no sense a book on cat care, the subject naturally comes up in its pages.

In different localities and over a period of more than twenty-five years, my husband and I have consulted numerous veterinarians. In quality they ranged from excellent to lethal. The superior ones were lifesavers, and we always tried to learn from them. I am thankful to those veterinarians who have helped us learn as we tried to do our best by our cats.

It is against this background of reading, inquiring, and caring for our cats that I have felt safe in including one or two comments of a medical or nutritional nature.

*To the ever green memory of all our dear
cats of yesteryear, to the four who live
with us now, and to all cats everywhere,
with love.*

Occasionally there come times when—against instinct and upbringing and beyond our means—I feel that my husband and I are making a vulgar display. Or would be making a vulgar display were anyone else present. In the absence of any other party there doubtless can be no more display than there is with that same old hypothetical and tiresome tree at the frozen North that is eternally falling, soundlessly because there is nobody there to hear it. Nonetheless, when all four cats are in the same room, I do feel rather like a woman who is wearing all her emeralds at once.

Exactly how our furred treasures feel about us is a secret that will have to remain locked in their hearts. In myriad ways, however, our cats show their feeling, unrolling it before us like a bolt of rich and subtly shaded silk. They come to meet us, sometimes at a lively clip. They run to us for protection. They lie on the desk while we work and on the ping pong table while we play. They take naps with us. They find the most rudimentary of small gardens transformed into Elysian Fields by the presence of even one of us, gardening or lolling in the shaded hammock; they gather round, they fan out, they come back singly and in pairs, they butt and nuzzle, they jump into but do not remain in the unstable hammock,

1

Sphinx of my quiet hearth!
Friend of my toil,
companion of mine ease...

GRAHAM TOMSON

Caressing rather than grooming is surely the idea when two already immaculate and *soigné* cats take turns washing each other.

A little lion, small and dainty sweet.

GRAHAM TOMSON

Gaylord does this intermittently and, even while temporarily hindering play, it pleases us all.

Some gracious instinct binds her to her home.
She feels the charms of the familiar,
and her fidelity to the sheltering hearth
has made her—now that
her old honours have passed away
—the little god of domesticity...

AGNES REPPLIER

they settle on nearby log, rock, or stone wall and stay for long periods. Gaylord expresses affection chiefly by being a genuine and dependable lap cat. In this regard, Grayling and Alan are sometimey. Trilby has other effective ways of making herself companionable.

She shined up one spring day for me when, for the sake of the bulbs and the next year's flowers, I went outside to cut dead daffodils. I had hardly begun when she joined me, although she had been in the house and I have no idea how she knew that when I left by the front door I wouldn't be in the car and long gone. She stayed with me for nearly an hour—observing my activities and occasionally rolling over and over to express her pleasure in spring sunshine plus open air plus fellowship. When I finished cutting the daffodils and pruning the crape myrtle I went to the back of the house, momentarily losing sight of her. As I proceeded, however, there she was jogging along beside me and there she remained until I finished my work and went back inside. Then she too came back into the house and resumed her nap in "her" Imari plate.

Often my husband and I go outdoors and see not one single solitary cat. As we take our narrowly circumscribed walk about the lot or do a chore or two connected with the planting, however, one by one they materialize. They romp with one another, gallop after small stones that we throw for them to chase, rub against us, investigate whatever we're doing and whatever we're doing it with; and Trilby is likely to plant herself on a rock or some other convenient perch for the duration, the very model of an interested spectator. Often she extends her interest to other people who are responsive or to situations she finds irresistible. Our builder, who later remodelled houses in the near vicinity, reported with pleasure that his little friend Trilby had "supervised" every job he'd done in the neighborhood.

Eyes that see and ears that hear are not everybody's, and they are no more likely to be the companions of total detachment than of excessive subjectivity. A sociologist, after cast-

Sometimes her ease and solace sought
In an old empty watering-pot,*
There wanting nothing save a fan
To seem some nymph in her sedan,
Appareled in exactest sort,
And ready to be borne to court.

WILLIAM COWPER

*A plebeian log holder will also serve.

When you notice a cat in profound meditation,
The reason, I tell you, is always the same:
His mind is engaged in a rapt contemplation
Of the thought, of the thought, of the thought of his name:
His ineffable effable
Effanineffable
Deep and inscrutable singular Name.

T. S. ELIOT

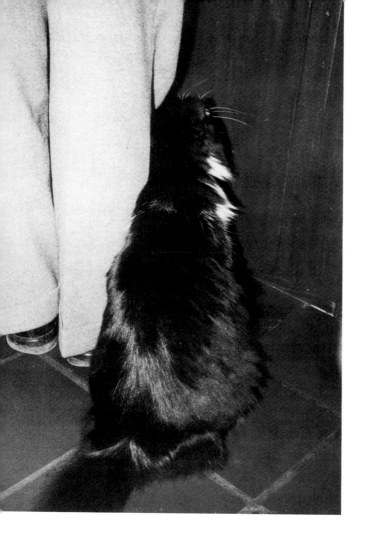

These legs are those of a friend of the cats, not of the surrogate parent who usually feeds them at night. Because he's accustomed to being cared for, however, Gaylord is touchingly confident that whoever is up there with access to the food is a potential surrogate parent and will give him his supper.

Food must be warmed, and they never receive it direct from the refrigerator. Nonetheless, our cats, as others, regard the refrigerator as a never-fail cornucopia on an equal with the can opener.

ing an impersonal eye on cats at mealtimes, tells us in a national magazine that, in a feeding situation, a cat relates to his owner less as a human provider than as a vestigial biological mother. I look at the cats through lenses different from his, and I don't see exactly that. If he means that the adult cat asks his owner for food in precisely the same way that, as a kitten, he asked his mother—but of course! (Cat owners have long known this, having learnt it from life experience and from reading about animals in the wild; so in some quarters it is called "folk wisdom.") If, however, he means to offer two contrasting or mutually exclusive concepts, the contrast is not apparent to some of us. What mother, surrogate or biological, would not be also provider? To our cats, I may indeed be the living emblem of the vanished feline mothers; but it is my own feeling that our cats regard me as all of a piece, human provider who is surrogate parent.

And the cats are right.

Certainly in a feeding situation, they "relate" to us by butting gently and stropping themselves against our legs, in the way the young of many mammals, including the canine wolves, ask their mothers and sometimes their fathers to give them food. But our cats very well *know* that my husband and I are their human providers. After all, they regularly and frequently accept provender (when it's acceptable) from our hands; and most of a certainty they know a cat when they see one, and realize that we are some other kind of being. We are sure that they also know that we are what can be called their surrogate parents, as they show a touching awareness that we take care of them in many ways additional to feeding. Pets, as differentiated from animals living in a state of nature and achieving independence in adulthood, become to a certain extent infantalized; and it seems their justified expectation to be permanently cared for by their owners. Cats, with impeccable logic, apparently subscribe to the concept that whoever takes care of you is your momma.

Cats have clearly discernible feelings toward people,

Deep in my brain walks to and fro,
As well as in his own domain,
A handsome cat of gentle strain,...

PIERRE CHARLES BAUDELAIRE

Gaylord's path crossed ours nearly four years ago at a time when we were petless and resolved to stay that way. Over a period of years we had had too many cats—acquired by rescue and, when healed or cured, immovably fixed in house and hearts—and we had been wrung by too many critical illnesses and finally deaths. There had been several deaths in rather short order just before we came catless to Washington, and we came in a grim and solid never-again state of mind.

We acquired the cats we have now one at a time and only one on purpose. Gaylord was five and a half months old. When it was put to us as a matter of us or the pound, our natural proclivities surfaced quickly and, without having had a look at him, all our granite determination turned to jelly. My husband, phoned in another state, said, "Well, go and *get* him." We believe that an animal should not be without at least one of his own kind, and we also knew that with his interim protector Gaylord had had the company of cats. It took us two months because, loath to invite further lacerations of our feelings, we were still dragging our feet; but we got Grayling for him. Trilby came the following June, and Alan last Christmas.

Gaylord is colored and marked in a way that was described by those undoubted catlovers Frances and Richard Lockridge as "black and white in odd places." The way we see it is that black-and-white is beautiful, no matter how bizarre the arrangement. Gaylord's fine coat is fluffy on chest and tail, he has an admirable head, yellow eyes, and a foaming cascade of shirtfront more dazzlingly white than that of *Showboat*'s Gaylord Ravenel. Melanism being what it is, his blackness is tinged with coppery overtones here and there. He is a large cat, tall and rangy but not heavy-boned. His purr is as small as his heart is big, and most often can be verified only by a finger on his throat. (His terrified purr, the purr used only rarely by any cats and then only in states of towering anxiety, is loud enough. I am inexpressibly grateful to him that his use of it alerted me to what had been happening at a hospital where I then found that humane agreements carefully made in advance had been deliberately and habitually broken. No cat of ours will ever be in that hospital again.)

At home, Gaylord is prepared to love all comers, and he doesn't seem to know that there are people in the world who wouldn't love him back. He reminds me of a line in a song Polly Bergen used to sing: "I will kiss anybody who will kiss me first." Except that Gaylord is more giving. He will love anybody who will so much as let him. If he's around when a visitor arrives, or, if outdoors he comes on us walking with someone else, he seldom fails to go first to that person and rub against the leg in greeting. It has happened too often, too regularly, to allow of any interpretation but that of welcome. He is babyish with us and motherly with the other cats. He is the mildest and gentlest of animals, and quite talkative. He has one peculiar utterance that delights us. This is a sort of musical buzz which functions as a simple and kindly acknowledgement, sometimes with a questioning intonation. This is voiced whenever we put a hand on him as we pass by.

14

He used to jump from the balcony deck across the thirty-seven-inch-wide stairs—a picayune jump except that it landed him on a two-and-a-half-inch ledge against the wall above the side of the staircase. He would then make his way along this precarious path—the stairs and quarry-tiled entry floor beneath—and on to a commodious deck with corner windows directly under the ceiling. Here, pleasurably high and with glass to the right of him and glass to the left of him, Gaylord could clearly see the next house, an intersection, and a little way down our street. We never knew what might have diverted him so much—His interest may well have been partly in the place itself—but we know that he observed the postman's stops across the street, people walking by, cars passing, delivery and garbage trucks on their rounds, neighborhood animals in their comings and goings. For at least two years Gaylord spent much time, day and night, in this special place of his. One year, when we had placed a Christmas decoration on the deck, we took his picture and used it for the next year's Christmas card. For a long time now, however, he hasn't given the place even a casual, offhand glance. This intense engrossment in a special little spot and then abrupt desertion of it is typically feline, but we miss seeing him up there.

Gaylord is like The Good Child in a family. He is a joy and a comfort, he scatters affection everywhere he goes, he is always available when one wants a cat to cuddle, and he frequently volunteers to cuddle with somebody. He is our first love (of this current pride), and we are utterly devoted to him. But it does sometimes seem that it's the others we talk about the most. Maybe it's that, unlike Trilby, he has never been at death's door; unlike Grayling, he is not timid and fearful; unlike Alan and Trilby, he has not had several narrow escapes from death by accident. Alone among the four, he has never once given us a sleepless night by staying out until morning. Alone among the four, he allows himself to be combed without behaving as if assault and battery and personal betrayal

Gaylord, reflective

Gaylord, antic

His tongue is sponge, and brush, and towel, and curry-comb,
Well he knows what work it can be made to do,
Poor little wash-rag, smaller than my thumb.

HIPPOLYTE TAINE

As do cats
in general,
Gaylord enjoys
the scents of
outdoors—earth,
grass, leaves,
flowers.

The only triple spoonfashion nap we've ever seen. It is no happenstance that Gaylord is in the middle. He is sending out vibrations of loving reassurance to Trilby and Grayling, and they are absorbing them and being nourished by them.

were under way. It is a temptation to say that he is simply no trouble, but that would not be true. Any pet who is really no trouble is a pet who is not being cared for. Gaylord is the regulation amount of "trouble," but he is never the wheel that gets the grease because it's squeaking.

Though he is the backbone of our pride, yet he is fleetingly overshadowed from time to time. He is not self-assertive, and he isn't quick to defend his rights; he'll allow Alan or any cat to nudge him away from his dinner plate (unless it's liver night). His manner is so modest that sometimes more ebullient personalities make more immediate claims on attention. Gaylord never remains in the background, however. As naturally and effortlessly as water seeking its level, he reassumes his front-and-center position. A paragon of patience, gentleness, and ever-ready affection, he is the one to whom all the other cats gravitate, and he is Number One not only by tenure but by popular acclaim.

Sometimes I think Gaylord is my favorite.

Sometimes an especially gentle
and loving male will appoint
himself surrogate mother
to a kitten.

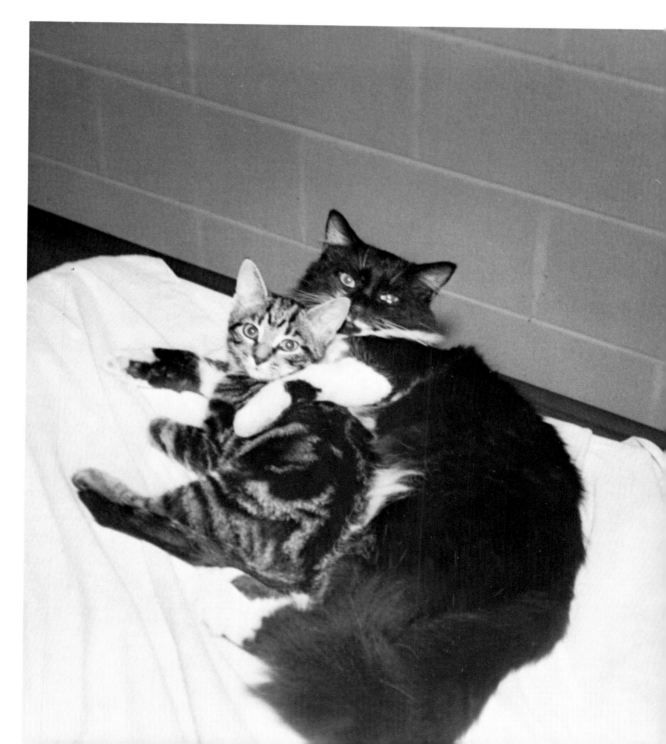

When we came home with the kitten for Gaylord on that October evening, there was instant uproar. Grayling was two months old, small for his age, scrawny and swollen from malnutrition, and more than half sick. Gaylord pounced on him the second he laid eyes on him. We were astounded at Gaylord, fearful for the kitten, and much harassed as we kept pulling Gaylord off the kitten or the kitten from under his suddenly huge paws. Finally my husband—It had been a long day—stamped upstairs saying, "I'm just going to count on Gaylord to do the right thing." I didn't actually think that

 Gaylord would kill the kitten for a mouse—although this is how it looked—but I did fear that he would do him considerable harm with rough handling and, to me, ambiguous intent. Then I noticed that when I separated them and set Gaylord down again, the kitten would go tottering straight back to him. The kitten had known all along that Gaylord was in transports of joy and love and entirely unable to keep paws or mouth off him. It was doubly well that we had acted on our strongly held principle that for an animal

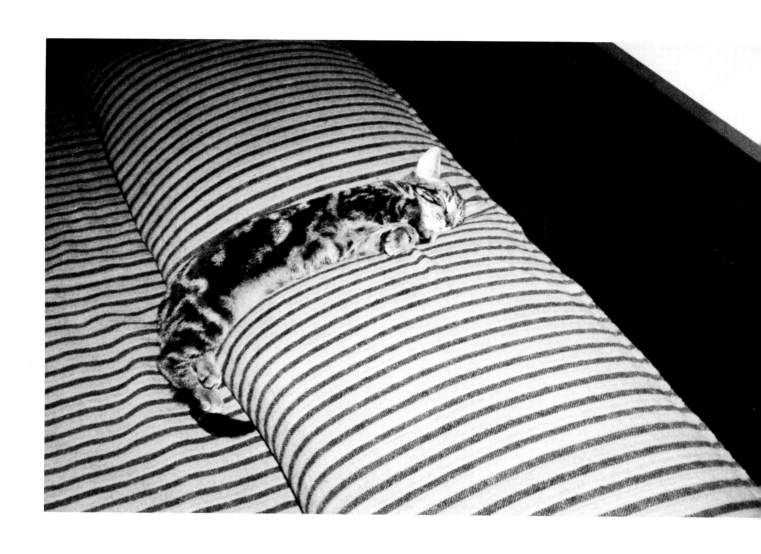

The cat in quiescence is medicinal to irritable,
tense, tortured men and women.

WILLIAM LYONS PHELPS

only is lonely; because even so we had failed to understand, and Gaylord had been powerless to explain, that in him the standard need was intensified to a desperate longing.

None of us got much sleep that night. We would all try to settle ourselves in bed, darkness and quiet would soothe us, and everybody, even Gaylord, would drift off. But Gaylord was far too excited for sleep to hold. All through the night he kept waking up and, rediscovering beside him the source of his all but unbearable happiness, pouncing yet once more on the unprotesting kitten. The next morning a more composed Gaylord, nearly eight months old and at that time a sexually intact male, was tenderly cuddling his precious waif under his long foreleg, the kitten clearly in paradise and Gaylord as self-satisfied and protective as any mother with her own baby.

The kitten, although reciprocally ecstatic in this familial arrangement, was after all not only young but weak and in need of rest; and he would occasionally flee Gaylord's sometimes oppressive attentions and seek cover under my breakfast tray. This was ineffectual because Gaylord would reach under and paw him out. For some days the only way the kitten was able to rest was to lie under the tray, which I walled up with a pillow on each side and which was by then a permanent fixture on the bed. In this little benign enclosure he could sleep the deep sleeps of infancy while Gaylord gazed longingly at him through the spokes at the ends of the tray stand. He gained strength by the hour, or so it seemed. He and Gaylord played as well as slept together, and their play was a most beautiful and affecting sight. Gaylord obviously appreciated the kitten's age and fragility and, even in the heat of the wildest romp, he never once failed to handle him as if he were made of tissue paper. We have one picture in which Gaylord appears to be gnawing on the kitten's narrow little chest; alarming at first glance, but the expression on the kitten's face is beatific. This first rapture moved into a halcyon period and then deepened into devotion that will endure as long as both cats are living.

With paw and eye
and posture, Grayling
tells a loved one of
his affection.

Their mutual devotion, begun when Gaylord adopted
Grayling at the age of two
months, has deepened into
a powerful attachment that
will endure as long as both
cats are living.

Kittens,…
If you'd grow to Cats respected,
See your play be not neglected.

OLIVER HERFORD

We can't give Grayling a "good greenwood," a cypress tree for his tent. But when he was two months old, we could give him a Norfolk Island pine in a pot. When he was four-and-a-half months old, we could give him a Christmas tree. Now in his beautiful prime, we can give him a Douglas fir outdoors.

Trilby and the others are perfectly willing to use their little private entrance when necessary, but they all much prefer to be let in or out doors or windows.

Safe within the house though they be, Grayling and Gaylord listen to an alarming sound outside and hold themselves in readiness for instant flight if it should become necessary.

When he was still new to us Grayling gave Gaylord a serious fright. When they first went outdoors together it was largely a straight case of monkey-see-monkey-do, but soon Grayling began to make tiny explorations on his own initiative. Then he became more ambitious. He noticed the white oak that stands cheek by jowl with the house at the back, and he saw that he could climb the trunk and then easily transfer to the roof. It was no sooner seen than done. We were mightily impressed with this enterprise and boldness in one whose age was still reckoned in weeks; but Gaylord, in the first flush, not to say throes, of his guardianship, was aghast. He plainly considered the kitten to be in mortal peril. He ran back and forth on the ground, alternately addressing the kitten and us in anguished and pleading tones, and he was not to be consoled until the kitten came down. This performance became less unnerving with repetition, and Gaylord steeled himself to make the tree-to-roof trip—solely, we believe, because the kitten continued to make it. With the act, his fears, for the kitten and for himself, vanished.

All our cats use the roof. They enjoy being up there, where they walk about, nap, take their ease, and observe the neighborhood scene. We live in a house of organic design, and the roof is only one of numerous features that couldn't be more suitable for cats' pleasure if they'd been planned for that purpose. The roof is on several levels, all readily accessible by tree or window. Our bedroom has an unenclosed window over one end of the living room, and this window has a reasonably cat-sized sill. There is not an upstairs hall, but a balcony over the living room. The balcony has a generous deck which is also the top of a bank of cabinets in the dining area, and this deck is in daily use as napping place and as vantage point from which can be seen entry, living-dining room, and, beyond that area's glass, outdoors to the back of the lot and beyond. There are no separate windowsills on the exterior, but a continuous sill running around the house, interrupted by spaces without windows and taking up again. There are other cat-pleasing

Oh, you who strive to relieve your overwrought nerves and cultivate power through repose, watch the exquisite languor of the drowsy cat and despair of imitating such restful grace.

AGNES REPPLIER

spaces and surfaces to be had for the finding. Our cats find them all, and these amenities seem to be much appreciated.

To pick up the thread again. Grayling has astonished us in more than one way, chiefly in his physical appearance and in one long unsuspected handicap.

My first glimpse of him was out of the corner of my eye from the window of the car as we drove down the main street of Culpeper, Virginia, on an afternoon's outing. My first thought was that there was a kitten we could probably get for Gaylord. I could see peripherally that there were other kittens and their mother, but Grayling, sitting in profile and with one paw playfully upraised to a sibling, was the one I noticed. This was one reason that we chose him when we returned a few hours later and effected the transfer; the other reason was that he was not afraid of us and the others were.

Safely resting beside my hand in the pocketbook on my lap, he purred all the way home. Even at a weak two months he had a big deep purr, and from that day to this he has purred almost every time either of us has touched him and sometimes if we've only looked at him or he at us. Sometimes in moments of shared affection, his purr takes on a higher, singing tone. He showed no fear of us on the day we got him or at any later time. To the contrary, he was plainly barefoot in clover from the moment of his arrival at home.

Our first surprise from Grayling was the change in his appearance, making his name an inappropriate name if there ever was one. As his body responded to good food and loving care, his natural colors came into their own and he turned into a rich lustrous black and tawny and buffy specimen of the kind called brown tabby, and he has long been considered the family beauty. The subtlety of his coloring and the complexity of his patterns are endlessly interesting. His coat is like a tapestry so lavish in detail that one could focus on almost any section and feast the eye. If the luscious color of his nose could have been mixed with pigments, they would have been salmon pink and a pinch of nutmeg brown.

Grayling is the splendid quintessential domestic shorthair, with the "mark of Mary" on his brow. (Legend has it that a cat came into the stable at a time when the infant Jesus was crying. The cat went to the Baby and comforted Him, and Mary, in gratitude and affection, reached out and stroked the cat. Under her touch the letter M appeared on its forehead, and it has appeared ever since on the forehead of every cat of this type.) His intricate markings, his colors, and his body build tally with descriptions of those of his remote ancestor the Egyptian cat. Such is the power of the heritage that the ancient markings, coloration, and conformation are the ones that occur most often in domestic shorthairs to this day.

Sad to say for his comfort and joy as he goes through life, Grayling later showed a grave handicap. He is mortally afraid of strangers. This came as a shock to us, because he had never seemed to regard us as strangers. As a two-month-old in rather desperate straits, he had, with seeming serenity, ridden thirty-five miles in a car with people he had never seen before. His outward behavior was more like that of a poor wandering one who had finally found his home and recognized it on sight than that of a kitten untimely removed from the bosom of his family.

He slowly improves, but this great fear is still with him. A loud heavy voice or an unfortunately piercing one, or any noise or quick movement will have him bolting from the room. Sometimes, when all is quiet and the unknown person does nothing to startle him, he holds his ground and seems to feel gratified by so doing. He dreads thunder, although to a somewhat lesser degree than in his younger days. When a squall is on its way, he's the first cat in the house, hurrying to see if we've left the right door open so that he can get under a bed if it becomes necessary. (We have.)

Grayling is bountifully loving by nature, but he has small scope for bestowing affection. He develops confidence in and fondness for any friendly person he sees often enough and long enough to feel familiar with; but his list of friends is a short one, because there are few he sees in the way that leads to achievement of friendship. Once firmly established, however, his regard endures even through rather long absences.

Grayling made two friends and lost them in the same way. One, who used to be frequently at the house, moved away and then came back after a year. Outdoors, he walked quickly through dead leaves toward Grayling, and the leaves made clattering sounds that frightened Grayling away. Less than ten minutes later, they met in the house. Grayling went straight to him and animatedly marched in place on the table while being petted, rubbed his head against his auld acquaintance, and generally carried on as we've never seen him do for anyone but ourselves.

Grayling's other friendship was fleeting because it was made in four consecutive evenings of concentrated effort and then unavoidably and suddenly broken off. Together, our out-of-state guest and Grayling had made marvelous progress, and before the guest left I took a picture of them snuggling on the sofa. I was puffed up with pride in both of them.

Both friends have been back, but after very long absences. For Grayling's sake we were saddened to see that he did not seem to remember them. Some worth-while residue of trust remained, however; he was considerably easier around them than he is around total strangers.

We will never know the cause of his sore affliction. It could be due to some maternal insult. (His three siblings were more heavily stricken than we later learned he is, and we have often wondered remorsefully about their fate), or it could have been the result of apparently never having had hunger and thirst fully satisfied during the entire first two months of his life. Or he may have had insufficient contact with other people during his first months with us. Or, or, or . . . It is idle to speculate, but we can't help worrying the subject from time to time.

Like many cats, Grayling has an aptitude for opening doors. Trilby paws nervously and haphazardly at doors or

Grayling has an incomparable belgard, the
look defined by Johnson in his dictionary as
"a soft glance, a kind regard." He shines on us.

windows to let it be known that she's exceedingly anxious to be let out, but Grayling often paws purposefully. He took note long ago when once or twice we failed to shut a door properly. His investigation showed that it only *looked* shut, and he pulled it open and went outdoors. Since then, when he's eager to go outside and we aren't co-operating, he feels it worth his while to try the doors. If he's accidentally given a little bit of a start, he can deal successfully with hinged doors, sliding doors, and folding doors.

Twice Grayling used a door in a way that astonished me. At a time when Alan was still weak from a severe illness, he stayed upstairs most of the time. Litter pans are in the basement, a long hike for a recuperating youngster; so I kept one upstairs for Alan. During the day, for the sake of appearances, I kept it in the study closet and he'd let me know when he needed it. Twice when it could have been nobody but Grayling, I found that he had opened the closet door and used the pan. Hardly noteworthy in itself; but, after leaving the closet, he had closed the door behind him. It is obvious that if a cat is upstairs it's far more convenient to have the facility right at hand than to trudge down to the basement, but I would give a pretty to know why Grayling felt called on to close the door when he left the closet after using the pan. He still occasionally opens this door and peers hopefully in—and, disappointed, leaves the door open.

He is not as consistently chatty as Gaylord, but as a communicator he is a nonpareil. More than once he has asked me to open an inside door simply by lightly placing one paw on the door and glancing up at me. No scratching at the door, no crying, no fidgeting, no ostentatious explaining of any kind. He knows that this spelling out behavior is unnecessary because I will understand him. Just the one token gesture and the one slight turn of the head will serve, and, by feline standards, less is more. Cats' every movement and their every message to sympathetic receivers illustrate what Chekhov said on a different matter: "When someone expends the least amount of motion on a given action, that's grace." All cats in motion are grace incarnate, and Grayling in communication as well.

He has an unparallelled belgard, the look defined by Johnson in his dictionary as "a soft glance, a kind regard." Konrad Lorenz has written of cats of Grayling's markings, "The striped markings in the face of the 'wild-colored' cat enhance the least movements of the facial skin and augment the vividness of the expression." Whether or not this accounts for it, Grayling's belgard is conspicuous among his charms. He shines on us. When he is feeling especially loving, and he often is, he can look at us and radiate almost palpable rays of pure tenderness. When he feels more effusive about it, he rolls over and over, using a universal feline mode of expression, and adds his own touch of all but standing on the back of his neck.

Just as we had not realized the depth of the young Gaylord's emotional need for another cat, we may be missing other important feelings impossible, for all their skill, for the cats to communicate. It may not be, as it seems to us, that Grayling is more than the others brimful of love and joy and profound gratification in home and associates that custom has not staled. They may be equally steeped in ever fresh loving contentment, but Grayling's almost visibly glosses him over with a bloom like that on grapes.

When he sleeps on the bed, and he often does, in the morning he wakes up purring. He appears to be as happy to see us as if we'd been separated for a week instead of for a night and that only by sleep. Occasionally he chooses to sleep under some piece of the bedroom furniture. On one memorable middle-of-the-night, I got out of bed. After I had groped my morose befuddled way half across the room in silence, my mood softened and lifted as I heard coming toward me out of the pitch black dark the steady vibrations of the rich and resonant purr that was Grayling's greeting.

He and Gaylord lavish affection on each other, much of it in the form of washing. Like all cats, they groom themselves almost compulsively, and this fervor is extended to their best friends. One cat licking his own coat is washing and preening, but petting more than grooming is surely the idea when two already immaculate and *soigné* cats take turns washing each other.

It is my impression that, to Gaylord, Grayling is still his kitten. It is also my impression that Gaylord washes Grayling a bit more than the other way around. They do take turns, however, and sometimes they wash each other simultaneously. During a mutual washing spree each maintains such an unflagging appearance of supreme happiness and contentment that it is plainly as rewarding to wash as to be washed.

Grayling took me by surprise when he was less than four months old by calling out when I came into a room where he was and he saw me first. He has continued to do this, a sweet and affectionate habit all his own. On one occasion, I was trying the excellent stretching and rolling exercises devised by the famous Miss Craig. I was lying on a heavy quilt on the floor alongside the daybed where Grayling was resting. For a few moments he observed with kindly interest the ludicrous spectacle of a human being stretching and rolling in the presence of a cat, whose species raised stretching and rolling to the level of an art. Then he joined me on the floor, lay himself down beside me, and stretched and rolled along with me for a few moments.

Sometimes I think Grayling is my favorite.

Like most cats, ours choose their own places to sleep.

They often find it pleasant to cram themselves into spaces not quite large enough or even distinctly uncomfortable.

. . . the wildest of tame animals and the tamest of wild ones.
LLOYD ALEXANDER

As with Trilby's eyeballing tactic, this little habit is pure bluff and all concerned know that. But the males give way, put up with it amiably, and bear her no grudge.

With a sheet of glass between them, young Alan gives freer rein to his sometimes anguished desire for Grayling to play with him. Without the kindly barrier, he would never hazard such an unrestrained gesture at such close quarters; and, even behind glass, it is rather coldly observed. When he feels rejected for too long, Alan picks a fight with Grayling. This will resolve itself in time.

In a typical feline exercise, Trilby exhibits an atavistic
caution in the presence of a strange object which may or
may not be alive and dangerous. A familiar enough object,

exciting no interest whatever when seen in its usual place, is by an unfamiliar placement transmuted into a potential danger and must be warily approached and tested.

Her tongue is thin, and can make a spoon of itself.

LEIGH HUNT

*Cats are quiet and graceful
animals, companionable
to men and women of
placid temperament and
a very real solace to those
of us who are irritable.*

MICHAEL JOSEPH

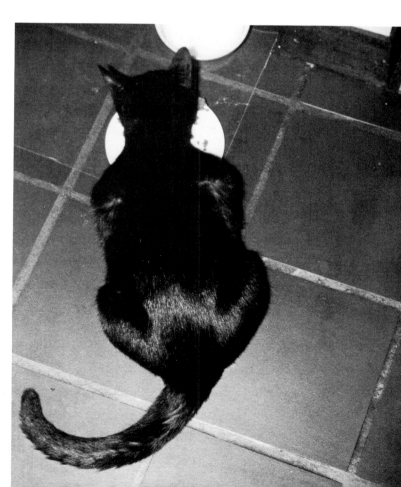

That they can "eat grass and get well" is a foolish figment and a dangerous one. Most cats do eat grass, however, given the chance, and many chew on houseplants. Amongst ours, Grayling is the plant eater. The jade plant and the Christmas cactus are favorites, being succulents, and he finds ferns irresistible. These are harmless, but much indoor greenery is not. Dieffenbachia, for example, is not called dumb cane for nothing; it is exceedingly toxic and its effect on the throat is agonizing. Toxicity should be kept in mind when buying houseplants; such information is not generally volunteered by sellers.

We took out the pads that go under table-
cloths and turned for one moment to put
them, still in a stack, on the table. We
turned back, and this is what we saw. It
required that, in one swoop, Trilby move
(up) from the passthrough and (over) into
this narrow slot of a shelf. How she inserted
herself into such a space—silently; no
scrambling—we cannot imagine.

Trilby is one of the pansy-faced cats; she has long and very thick fur and a great plume of a tail. Her coat is mainly an unassuming gray, giving her at first glance the demure look of a nineteenth century novel's heroine—a young person of impressive personal excellence but of no means, whose best  dress is always dove gray. Trilby's eyes are green as grapes, the silken fur on her chest is a froth of snowy jabot, and on her underside there are large splashes of buff. She is tremendously spirited and she has a face of rare sweetness.

That's Trilby today. When she came to us, her fur, in ruins from near-starvation, was dry as a chip and consequently so stiff that it stood straight out from her emaciated body. This made her look like a hefty little barrel, but when I picked her up it was like lifting a cigarette paper. Her eyes were big as dinner plates and staring with anxiety, and her face was drawn and pinched. On each side of her neck the fur had disappeared, leaving two large areas of skin as bare as that on a human neck. In these undefended areas seven ticks were embedded, gorged on her blood. She had obviously been a pet, showing a ready trust in strangers that has to be so learned. When she was invited into a strange house by well-spoken strangers, she was so responsive that we felt in her a significant measure of relief and the most touching expectation that from that moment on things were going to be all right.*

The ticks gave us pause. We knew that in her ravaged condition she could ill afford yet another painful experience and that if we hurt her in getting out the first tick it would be difficult and distressing to get out the others, and we would have undermined her immediate confidence in us. Still, it was imperative that we get them all out, and without breaking heads off in her flesh to cause festering wounds. We did all the things we were told to do, and met with total failure. Then I was smitten with the idea of anesthetic ointment. My husband went on the double to the nearest drug store and returned with a tube of cream. I squeezed this copiously around and over each tick in turn, waited ten to fifteen minutes, and, with my fingers protected by facial tissue, lifted out each one as smoothly as thread off a spool. Trilby didn't bat an eye. Her skin was anesthetized and she hadn't felt a twinge. I kept running with one unlovely little package after another to where my husband waited with a magnifying glass. Each tick was found to be intact, with head in place.

Good feeding soon restored fur to those initially bare places, but Trilby continued to growl when handled. Growling is a standard response to pain, but the doctor we had then kept insisting that nothing was wrong. We ourselves were mystified, because all during this time she frequently ran and played with the other cats as if she hadn't an ache or a pain. I learnt later that this is a typically deceptive characteristic of

---

*In a condition of need, a cat who has been a pet—and whose reverses have not included open abuse—will regard any person as potential provider and surrogate parent. This can be the most pitifully and painfully mistaken notion of a pet's life—It may even cost her her life—but experience has been her teacher, and she will so regard any person who does not demonstrate contrariwise and in a way she recognizes. (A crime of omission, such as an owner's failure to provide necessary medical attention, brings suffering without recognition of cruelty; and an abandoned cat is not physically afraid of kindly strangers if the desertion was perpetrated without surface violence.)

her ailment. A year later, when she was laid low and trembling all over with pain, a new doctor made a diagnosis. She had a Vitamin E deficiency of formidable but not yet lethal proportions, caused by near-starvation and, for all we knew, an all-fish diet before that. Over a period of months, daily cortisone tablets gave quick, almost magical, relief from pain while Vitamin E was replaced in her starved body. With recovered health, her eyes became eye-sized, her face relaxed into its natural shape, and her fur became glossy and smooth. Under all that luxuriant fur she's a light-boned cat.

The other cats make a fine foil for her unmistakable femininity. She sits with her front paws neatly together, so exquisite and so reserved that it's more than a touch startling when suddenly she's wrestling. Never mind that she looks like an embattled mimosa blossom; she wrestles competently. She can't actually hold her own with the heavier males; but she has developed some ingenious feints, she knows more about psychological warfare than the three of them put together, and she manages to give a pretty good account of herself. She has a strong will and nobody will ever hypnotize *her*, but her feet are surely as pretty as the fabled feet of du Maurier's Trilby.

As a rule, Trilby makes her most common wants known in the usual feline way of rubbing against legs and leading to the appropriate spots. Sometimes, however, when she urgently needs a snack or a door opened, all her ingrained feline refinement of manner deserts her. If we are in the bedroom and she well knows it, she doesn't climb the stairs, as the others would, to present her request. This lass with the delicate air—and *really* she has a most delicate air—stands at the foot of the stairs and screams. Trilby is the one and only party from whom I will accept being hollered at from one room to another.

When she plodded into our yard that broiling June evening, it was painfully clear that Trilby had at one time been a pet, that she had wandered unfriended for a long way and a

3

1

2

4

5

48

Never Susannah (while the Elders peered
Into the mysteries of her bath) was more
Unconscious of an audience.

MAZIE V. CARUTHERS

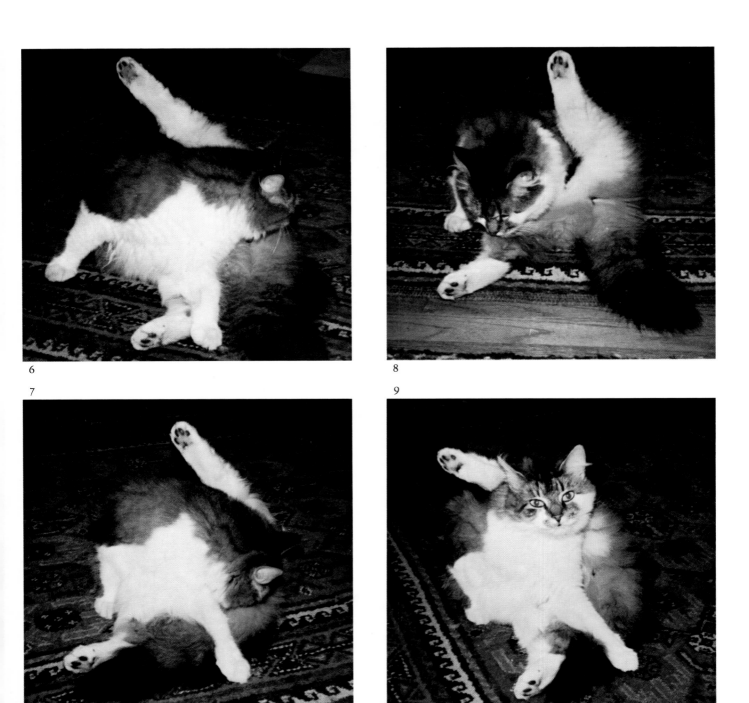

6

8

7

9

long time, had been through the mill, and was in a bad way. She had been in the house for two hours before she knew there were other cats here, and, in her devastated condition, Gaylord and Grayling came as a nasty surprise she was in no way fit to cope with. When she saw them she growled and screamed horribly. They too were taken by surprise, and they replied in kind.

Before long a beautiful thing happened. Not happened. Before long Grayling did a beautiful thing. He did it several times over, leaving in my mind's eye a picture preserved as if in amber. He would approach Trilby slowly and with great good will written in every line of face and body. Poor Trilby, physically and emotionally exhausted, and, we learnt belatedly, hurting all over, would hold her ground and hiss and spit. Confronted with this noisy and point-blank animosity (It was the face that fear put on), Grayling would continue without pause until he was within leg's length of Trilby. He would then sink to his side, in a position from which no attack could possibly be launched, duck his perfect head, look meltingly up at her, and speak in a cooing trill. Only a cat of stone could have resisted him, and our Trilby is by no means a cat of stone. In less than two weeks, shaky though she was, they were frisking about together, entirely at ease with each other.

Trilby is the most featherfooted and precisely balanced of cats. What in another cat would be jumping to a table top is in her something more like levitation. Although she is not a long-leggity cat, she's a great jumper; and this skill stood her in good stead once when she was, as the saying goes, between a rock and a hard place.

The extended window sills around the exterior of our house are used by all our cats for entering and leaving the house by windows, and their corners for sitting and surveying the surroundings. One of our bedroom windows is the customary upstairs entrance-exit. The first day Trilby came around the corner of the house, she saw me in the bedroom and asked to be let in the window. Unfamiliar as she was, she walked on past the movable window and found, as she stood on the three-inch ledge, that (1) the ledge stopped at a wall, (2) she was alongside a stationary glass window, (3) she was facing in the opposite direction for entering the movable window, and (4) thirteen feet below was a concrete pavement. Right before my eyes she took stock of the situation and, not moving out of her tracks, she arched her back and shot straight up into the air for more than a foot and a half, did an aerial about-face and landed featly on the ledge, the whole brilliant maneuver conceived, planned, and executed almost in the blink of an eye. It was impossible for me to dwell on the beauty of this exploit with my heart in my mouth, and if it had been possible it would be to my discredit; but I noticed it tangentially and, recollecting in comparative tranquility, I know it to have been in and of itself a compellingly beautiful performance of a virtuosa.

I opened the window with unsteady hands, eager to snatch her in and hug her. But, cloaked in dignity, she leisurely and daintily stepped through the window, so elaborately casual, so cool that butter wouldn't melt in her mouth. She was behaving as if this were the way everybody entered windows. Faced with this consummate aplomb and throw-it-away artistry, I felt obliged to suppress my impulse to unseemly display.

This sensational leap was not a conscious bravura affair but altogether an act of emergency. Cats characteristically exert just what effort is absolutely necessary for a given purpose, that and no more; and, as all the world knows, therein lies the beauty of their movement. It's as the child in the joke said about the right change: It's all there, but just barely. In a strange and plainly perilous situation—Yes, *I know* they land on their feet, but they are flesh and blood and bone and not shockproof—Trilby had almost instantly grasped the problem and worked out a perfect solution. To negotiate the great leap upward, she had made a split second decision to err on the safe side, simultaneously taking the ledge's measure for future

With Alan and Trilby,
peek-a-boo is invitation
and prelude to a chase,
after which they come
back to the starting place
and begin all over again.

They both enjoy
basic peek-a-boo
with people.

reference and factoring in that it was up against a stationary glass window. With all these mental calculations at her paw tips, she has since been able to manage without putting herself to the rigorous exertion required by the fireworks. She has never—no, not once—repeated the electrifying feat, because there has been no need. Later, the situation was no longer one of emergency but one of known risk cancelled by a known safeguard.

When she occasionally walks past the window now, it's her way of telling me that she really wants to come in and isn't merely loitering out there as they all are at times. Then, with the uttermost nonchalance, she ever so slightly raises herself on her hind feet, pivots in a semi-circle (toward the glass always), just clears the sill with her front feet, and presto, chango! she's exactly in position to enter by the window. This too is a lovely maneuver, small and subtle and economical, and, while equally dangerous, somehow easier on the nerves of the observer once one gets used to it.

Trilby is eloquently expressive of her affection, which is considerable, but she is not as free as the others to maintain close physical contact. Her first twelve to twenty-four months are a mystery to us and have left marks on her that puzzle and pain us. I never before knew a cat who didn't almost as a matter of course jump onto a bed the minute it saw one. It took months of coaxing to get Trilby on the bed at all, but we coaxed her assiduously because we wanted her to be relieved of her manifest fear. Whatever monstrous treatment had made her afraid to be on a bed had combined with two years of pain from undiagnosed and therefore progressively worsening illness to bring about continued fear of being on the bed and the risk it brought of close physical contact. Now, as the healing hand of time cleanses and closes psychic wounds and her physical illness has been vanquished, she nonchalantly jumps on the bed rather frequently and shows her pleasure at being there. More often she clears a space for herself on one of the bedside tables and sleeps there all night.

Often in the small hours I rouse a bit and I feel Trilby close against my foot or at my side. (The only cats I've known before who would snuggle beside a person only when she was lying flat and still and probably asleep, and therefore unable to make any sudden move, were terribly timid at the time.) Trilby is hardly afraid of us, but some of her pain-engendered fear behavior has outlasted the once chronic pain. It does seem that when I'm asleep she figures it's highly unlikely that I'll rise up and thrust pills down her throat or do any of the other unpleasant things that I've done from time to time, or unwittingly hurt her by handling her. No, she's not timid, but experience has made her quite skittish about what we might do in these painful or otherwise objectionable ways and she's not having any more of that if she can help it. She occasionally jumps on the bed when I'm there and awake and sitting up, and this delights me. Sometimes at night I stir in my sleep and feel an airy-fairy weight land on the bed, and I know that Trilby is there. One night she kneaded my pillow—made biscuits, as I called it in my childhood—settled herself, and took a long nap beside my head. I went back to sleep feeling as if I'd been decorated.

One of the most winning things about this winning little cat is the big welcome. My husband counts that day lost that she isn't outdoors when he comes home from work; because, hearing the car, she rushes around the house to the driveway for an extravagant spectacle of exuberant rolling and rolling in overjoyed welcome. (I too get the rolling ovation if I'm returning after an absence of several hours.) Nowadays we both arrive in the car because I've been to the bus stop to meet my husband, and Trilby always does for him what Gaylord does for company: She directs her first greeting to him, and I come in a poor second. I've been home all day, he's been gone all day, and he's the one she's joyous about.

At such times Trilby is almost sure to allow herself to be picked up and hugged and to enjoy it, provided we don't overdo it. Her receptivity and response to affectionate han-

One of the most delightful aspects of living with a cat is the cat's serene conviction of equality.

MARGARET COOPER GAY

Oh, cat, I'd give all Gilead's balm,
To have your cat-aleptic calm!

SAMUEL HOFFENSTEIN

dling are in direct ratio to her degree of relaxation. Half asleep or relaxed by physical activity or the benison of outdoors (and doubtless having run it through the computer in her head that we've never attempted medication or other indignities outdoors), she purrs her tiny purr and nuzzles and luxuriates briefly in being held. Trilby has many a deep hurt to overcome, but her essential nature is warmly loving.

Trilby is saucy and touchingly sweet and vulnerable in a most beguiling mixture. Despite the delicacy of her structure and appearance and her singular sweetness, she is a spicy one and she's what a European friend used to call "alert to insult." When she feels that a liberty has been taken, she's very sharp with the other cats or with us—or when, for some reason unknown to us, she feels moved to remind one of the other cats what's what around this establishment. In the latter circumstance she darts at the hapless male, brakes to an abrupt crouching halt squarely in front of him, and eyeballs him. This maneuver holds a strong element of psychic attack, as to be eyeballed by Trilby is, for a cat of any sensibility whatever, a discomfiting experience. It's pure bluff and all concerned know that, but the males give way, put up with this more or less amiably, and bear her no grudge. This is as it should be, because sweet-and-pungent Trilby, quick as she is to resent any trespass against her person or her dignity, simply is incapable of remaining cross for more than ten minutes. This endearing trait makes us all amenable to her seeming capriciousness. Moreover, she has a distinct aura of poignancy that makes me and my husband exceptionally tender of her feelings. Once, because we had guests at dinner, I was sitting at the end of the table in the chair we all recognize as Trilby's chair and not my usual place at the table. I went to get something from the kitchen, and when I came back one minute later she was comfortably settled on her chair. Without hesitation or ado, I gently shifted her position and sat on the edge of the chair for the rest of the meal and the others at the table none the wiser. It was, after all, her chair; and she was more sharing it with me than I with her.

She and Gaylord are quite chummy and we frequently see them strolling outdoors or coming into the house together. She plays well with Grayling, and I do hope she remembers that it was Grayling who came hurtling from the other side of the lot to drive away a strange cat who was chasing her. Grayling had been resenting this cat as an intruder, but had never dared to accost him until he chased Trilby. With Alan, she plays boisterously. Alan is still young and extremely sportive. For a couple of months he was pestilential in his attentions to the patient Gaylord, but matters have been somewhat eased for Gaylord now that Trilby plays with Alan so wholeheartedly, so often. For his size, Alan is an incredibly heavy cat, and in play the roughest we have ever had. We find it remarkable and moving that the small frail anxious Trilby understands that his rough-tough behavior will never result in intentional hurt. She does a lot of screaming at close quarters, for which she can hardly be faulted (So does big Gaylord), but she has no fear of Alan and the chasing and racing and wrestling go right on.

They have long had a game, one part tag, one part hide and seek. It is played with dining table and chairs, Trilby on the table and Alan underneath. How they formed rules and agreed on roles is anybody's guess, but they began playing the game when Alan was a newcomer and they still play it in just the same way. Alan moves from chair to chair and, rarely, when insupportably pressed, on the floor, all around the table. It hardly seems fair for him ever to take to the floor where she couldn't possibly reach him, bound as she is to remain on the table; but he has only been momentarily carried away, and he's quickly back up on a chair and the game goes on. Trilby rushes about in short dashes on the table top, trying to catch him. Occasionally he tries to halt fleetingly in an undiscovered spot, but this is only an effort to confuse her; generally he keeps on the move. His job is to change places as rapidly and with as little sound as possible. Her job is to locate him

To be free in outdoor surroundings blesses them with a sense of well-being unobtainable from any other source.

and to tag him. She leans way over the table's edge, swinging her foreleg from the shoulder, while Alan nimbly pops over to another chair.

Tagged or untagged, he keeps moving and she keeps pursuing. They never swap positions. It's a fast game and soon over. They stop as if at a prearranged signal noticeable only to themselves, and I have never seen either cat attempt to keep the game going after quitting time has come.

The only kind of appeal we see in Trilby is powerful, but her magnificent spirit is overwhelming. When she first came into our house out of the broiling June evening I have mentioned, she was not only exhausted and emaciated but stricken by the special kind of horror that afflicts a pet who finds herself homeless and wandering and suffering without recourse. Our guest, meaning nothing better or worse than common civility, leaned from his chair and reached out to her. This registered on Trilby as a threat. Ravaged but not shattered, this stouthearted little cat rose to her hind feet and clapped her front paws smartly together twice in rapid succession right under his nose.

Once when she was again a pet—Oh, a pet!—she was sitting on the passthrough between the kitchen and the dining area, and seemed to be coming over to the kitchen counter where I didn't want her to come. Waving my hand backward from the wrist, I made a frankly fake shooing motion. As if by reflex, her paw flashed out in a make-believe blow at the offending hand. Neither of us touched the other and neither had the remotest intention of so doing, but: I'd been rude to her; she'd be rude to me. In a small creature who had fairly recently known shock and terror as well as considerable and prolonged physical pain, this spirit staggers us and leaves us lost in admiration.

We do not harbor the unrealistic expectation that Trilby will ever be quite the cat she could have been, given a less harsh and arduous former existence. Still, she blooms as the rose—not as the showy and sculptured hybrid tea, but as the appealing and matchlessly fragrant old damask.

Even though I am writing about Trilby and other individuals and not The Cat, there is something that must be said for Trilby and for all cats. As the Jain teaching rightly has it, all creatures wish to avoid pain, all creatures long to live. Some are more tenacious of life than others, and among these the fierce tenacity of cats is proverbial. The smallest kitten, if given proper medical attention and cared for encouragingly, can bring awe-inspiring resources to the fight against sickness or injury. These inner resources are called into action, though doubtless with less potency, when a luckless cat is obliged to survive or not as he can without moral support. Trilby, who often seems to me to be a vivid distillation of universal feline qualities, provided impressive evidence of this will to live. During the extended period when she was performing latter-day feats of courage and tenacity—Earlier and more valiant feats were performed when alone, lost, and starving and with nothing but raw courage to draw on—she had long been named Trilby. We had not then heard a Yoruba myth about crimson cloths and a man, Onigbori, who lifted up his head and came back from death. But now it occurs to me that there is this that must be strongly put about Trilby: *She lifts up her head.* She is not indestructible, as the unknowing and uncaring seem to "think" about cats; she is as vulnerable as any; but she lifts up her head. We could not have named her Onigbori; it comes too haltingly from American tongues. We could not have named her Phoenix even; it is too grand for an appealing furred friend who is physically small. Both are too exotic for comfortable everyday use. "Trilby" does nicely, but we are ever aware that it is a superficiality. Under that delectable exterior, saved from candy-box prettiness by character, she is Trilby, she is Phoenix, she is Onigbori.

Sometimes I think Trilby is my favorite.

The cat is an individualist, the aberrant;
he is the creature who has never
run in packs nor fought in herds
nor thought in congregations.

FRANCES AND RICHARD LOCKRIDGE

Alan began to enliven our household immediately after Christmas. To leave aside the larger elements of an unhappy chain of events, we picked up and brought home, sight unseen, a young cat who had weighed on us ever since we'd known he'd been found crying in the snow in our neighborhood and hustled off to the pound. Although I phoned while he was being taken there and made arrangements for him to be brought to me, a mistake was made and he disappeared into the maw of the shelter. He then became "the county's property" and I was refused him until a representative came to inspect us, our cats, and our premises. In itself, such inspection is not only absolutely right but indispensable. Nine days went by, however, before this inspection took place. During that time, the young cat, healthy when delivered to the shelter, caught there a respiratory ailment and was exposed to the wildly infectious feline distemper. Our veterinarian warned us that his condition endangered his life and the lives of Gaylord, Grayling, and Trilby as well. Our only weapons against incipient disaster were fresh

Sometimes they will
sleep in places especially
provided for them.

booster shots (which are not instantaneously effective) for the three already at home and serum inoculation and isolation for the newcomer.

When we reached home and opened the wicker hamper, up stood a seven-month-old catling, long and narrow, black and shiny as licorice, yellow eyed, ravishingly beautiful, bursting with affection, and burning with fever. In order to save him from the usual fate at the pound I had signed a promise to keep him, but we had meant to enlist the help of a private organization that seeks homes for homeless animals. Our best laid and honorable though disingenuous plans went completely awry, however, because we had him to nurse for a month. This involved antibiotics on schedule round the clock, medication for an ailment induced by antibiotics, feeding milk-egg-yolk-sugar mixture with a tiny syringe, the whole catalogue.

When he began to be able to eat—first baby food meat from a fingertip, then from a plate—he was kept isolated in the study; the contagion still threatened the other cats. Even in a pleasant room with windows on the street, isolation is no small matter for an animal who has already spent nine hungry and anxious days in a pound atmosphere and who gives every evidence of having been a pet. (Advertisements and inquiries proved fruitless.) He was desperately affectionate, possibly because so badly shaken by the pound experience, and he needed much demonstrative response to allay his insecurity. Each of us spent as much time as possible in the study. Many an evening my husband napped there, his feet on an ottoman, his chair tilted far back, and small Alan curled up asleep on his chest.

We were undone by the extended stint of nursing plus Alan's obvious anxiety and need, and also he was a charmer. We are both constitutionally unable to care for a sick animal for any such period of time and then give him away. I kept asking, "Who will give him yoghurt tablets when he has to take antibiotics? Who will give him calcium-and-magne-

Whoe'er you be, for many centuries now
You've shared our milk and also caught our mice,
And yet you have not changed a single "miau",
Or taken on one virtue or one vice.

WILLIAM WALLACE WHITELOCK

Sometimes restraint crumbles before Alan's gleam and glitter, and there is nothing to do but gush that he looks like a jewelry cat—all citrine eyes and sculptured black basalt glass.

. . . . *dignity and freedom of spirit . . . . intelligence and grace . . . . companionship and consolation . . . . But these are ideas we can understand by words. At bottom, cats are like music. The reasons for their appeal to us can never be expressed too clearly.*

LLOYD ALEXANDER

My kitten's tender paw, thou soft, small treasure . . .

HEINRICH HEINE

The night exerts a powerful
pull on cats, who are, after all,
nocturnal by nature. In the main,
they tolerate quite well the
reversal of their sleep cycle to
coincide with that of people's.
We always know, however, that
there will come a few balmy
evenings in early summer when
one of ours will find it
impossible to give up the night,
and will refuse to show up, let
alone come inside, until morning.

sium in his food to stave off arthritis when he's older? Who will . . .?" And answering myself, "Nobody." Of course I know that's wrong. There are surely multitudes who do much more; but by that time we were both hopelessly entangled and thoroughly, if mistakenly, convinced that nobody would take as good care of him as we would.

For numerous reasons we fervently wanted not to have a fourth cat. Three is the ideal number, and we were fatly satisfied with our little group as then constituted. We gave more than a passing thought to medical fees. We feared the risk of disruption. Gaylord had found the addition of Trilby so hurtful that he quit sleeping on our bed. That selfsame Gaylord who had never slept anywhere else since the first night he spent in this house didn't sleep on our bed for three months. He was his usual dear self with one crucial exception: He didn't sleep on the bed. He was never sulky or grouchy; it's not in his nature; he just didn't sleep on the bed. We and Gaylord and Trilby had finally prevailed over that circumstance, and we shrank from another threat to the common weal. Gaylord and Grayling, without benefit of Polonius, continued to grapple each other to their souls with hoops of steel. We quailed all over again at having this bond tested a second time, and the alarmingly attractive Alan already doted on Gaylord. Nevertheless, here Alan was, we nursed him, he flourished, he was ours, and we were his.

Alan was soon effervescent, fairly aquiver with life. Before he was well enough to have the run of the house without further endangering the health of the other cats, he was a marvel of good temper if not patience about being kept in one room; but he was incessantly wanting and needing to play. In the absence of an obliging cat, my husband or I would serve. Alan had little games of hiding and pouncing and tackling ankles as we walked by pretending we didn't know he was around. We tried in our ponderous human way to hide and pounce, and he gladly changed roles, scurrying frantically and delightedly when it was his turn to be taken by surprise. When

71

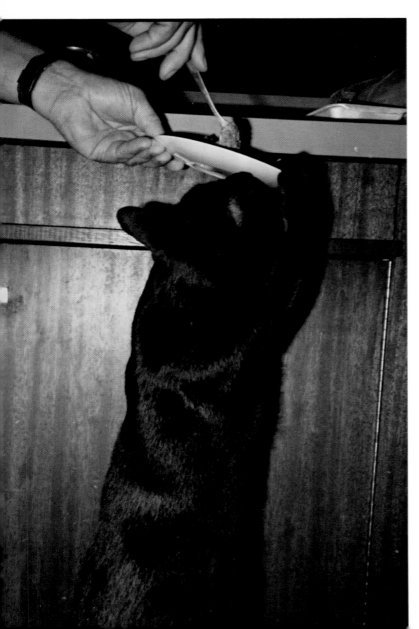

Trilby, Grayling, and Gaylord are eager but composed as they watch their supper of raw beef kidney being placed on plates. Alan isn't always able to be patient, perhaps because of youth, perhaps because patience isn't particularly in order at a given moment. It may be that this meal is late.

we swung a tapemeasure, he made the highest widest handsomest leaps we've ever seen. I don't know about lords, but one cat a-leaping like Alan is breathtaking. When, as his zeal caused to happen numerous times, he'd crash into the wall and plummet to the floor, he would pick himself up and rush back to the game without missing a beat.

Another small game similar to tackling was one I had played with Gaylord when he was only and lonely. (An only cat *must* be played with.) It began by my approaching Alan's face with the fingers of one hand spread as if to grasp his whole head. When the lowering hand reached a certain point, he'd leap from the floor, clutch my forearm with both forelegs, and swing. He and I enjoyed this, but both of us knew that he was only making do. As soon as he was a free agent, our rather scratchy game was discontinued. I remember that one day I suddenly realized that we didn't play it any more. I had stopped without thinking as Alan busied himself in hot and happy pursuit of Gaylord. For a few weeks thereafter he frequently woke all of us during the nights, pestering the other cats to play with him. A cat advanced on by Alan with play in mind had several choices: escape him, clobber him, play with him. Generally they preferred not to clobber him.

When he was well enough to go outdoors, he had the adventure of following his beloved Gaylord to the rooftop. Then, treat upon treat, he discovered the continuous sill that goes more or less around the house. This excited his interest to such a pitch that he spent a good part of that early afternoon going rapidly round and round the house by way of this ledge and the oak tree, and he kept me busy opening and closing windows as he went in and out of them repeatedly. He was so young and so newly cured and freed, and everything was a discovery and nearly everything a joy.

The first time he saw us playing ping pong he tried to join in. He was spectacular, making nine consecutive leaps in rapid succession back and forth over the net in pursuit of the ball. Then he saw that things were hopelessly against him, and he gave up the jumping and never did it again. He lay on the table as we played, though. For several weeks he would reach out from his recumbent position and swat at the ball whenever it passed him closely enough. Sometimes we stopped our own game for one of us to send a ball across the net to Alan. He would try to hit it (or did he try to catch it?) and quite often succeeded in hitting it back across the net. Trilby had done something of the sort the first time she saw us playing, but, being older and wiser, she had stopped after three jumps over the net. Later she would occasionally lie on the table while we played, as Gaylord often does.

Now at eleven months Alan has become less of a small hurricane, but he brims over with animal spirits and he plays hard. He clearly revels in everything around him. He relishes his meals (On the rare occasions when he doesn't, he lets us know in the time honored way), he rejoices in the other cats, he loves to disport himself outdoors, and he's quite affectionate with us. His affectionate displays are losing the quality of desperation, but he remains demonstrative. The overall impression he gives is of openness, alertness, eagerness, and guileless good will and good cheer. For this last engaging quality we gave him his name, meaning "cheerful", deciding against the similar Hilary as not suitable for an American cat.

When he goes outdoors and I see him springing across the lot to run up to a tree, stand on his long hind legs and hug the tree insofar as his physical limitations allow . . . When I see him and the others rolling voluptuously in earth or grass, sniffing growing things or holding up their heads on stretched necks to catch the varied outdoor scents the breezes bring . . . I realize all over again that if animals do not, like Antaeus of old, draw strength directly from Mother Earth, they do so indirectly. To move freely in outdoor surroundings blesses them with a sense of well-being unobtainable from any other source, and to be denied this is a severe deprivation.

As Alan's health returned he became combatively male, eager to pass the inexperienced stage without any

The door stands open in invitation to the outdoors unavailable to him during a long illness,
and he is scarcely more than a kitten. But little
Alan's all-feline nature dictates caution when
confronted with something, no matter how
tiny, unidentifiable. He investigates it in
exactly the way that is standard procedure with
all cats.

shillyshally if possible. It certainly wasn't possible here, as we view with horror and anger the catastrophic production of kittens caused by irresponsible owners who fail or refuse to have their cats spayed or castrated. For this human crime countless cats are killed every day, many horribly and there is no nice way, in pounds all over the country. (The yearly average is seven million two hundred thousand.) Our hearts sink when we hear from people who "wanted her to have one litter" or felt that it would be "good for the children." From one male and one female of that one litter astronomical numbers of foredoomed kittens could issue, and I despise the attitude that animals are educational toys. When I hear the line about having "found homes for all of them", I retch. This solves that one wilful *owner's* problem, but it exacerbates the hideous fate of cats unpardonably.

To return to Alan. When his upsurging maleness was becoming disturbing to him and to all of us, a hectic period followed, as he had to have a little time to regain full health and strength before undergoing general anesthesia and surgery. At that time of confused turbulence, he didn't seem to realize that Gaylord is a male. Trilby was non-violent but firmly and petulantly aloof and Alan got the message. He knew very well that Grayling is a male, and his unalterable policy was, "Attack! Attack! Attack!" Small and immature as his kitten's body was, propelled by inner tumult he was formidable. Once during a vigorous attack I separated them by picking Alan up and starting upstairs for his old room, the study. Half way there I let go.

I could no more have continued to hold him than I could have held an exploding firecracker. He burst from my hands. Because he was still laying about him in all directions even as he was falling, his claws caught in the skirt of my woolen bathrobe and for a few moments he swung in wide arcs, his orangy-yellow eyes blazing up at me from his rather sharp little inverted triangle of a face. Freed from my robe, he tore back downstairs in his singleminded harassment of

Alan is not, as the expression goes, "sharpening his claws." Cats' claws, as snakes' skins, loosen and must be shed. Here Alan is working to rid himself of loosened claws and to free the new ones waiting underneath. Cats give every appearance of pleasure in this task, and perform the exercise whether or not the state of the claws calls for it.

Grayling. They had to be separated quickly before one or both were mauled, and there wasn't time to fetch something made of lightweight cloth to throw over them. I herded Alan up the stairs and into his room by gently sliding a broom along the floor against him, Alan retreating in splendid order—stepping backwards and fighting the broom tooth and claw every inch of the way. After a short time alone, relieved of the infuriating sight of Grayling, he was once more mild as a moonbeam.

Alan's furore was the standard condition of the antagonized burgeoning male. When an intact male is worked up to the point of serious fighting, the entire world falls away from him. There is nothing on earth but the fight, and if the adversary is removed he will fight whatever is within reach. He has no choice. At the mercy of hormones rampaging through his system, a kitten-cat will rashly attack even an intact and mature male who could make mincemeat of him with one paw behind his back.

Mother Nature, that cruel wastrel, is interested only in survival of species to the total disregard of individuals. She *wants* litters of kittens, regular as clockwork, and she cares not how many die or exist in misery just so that enough survive long enough to serve her purpose. Her plan is draconian in its effect on male, female, and offspring, but she doesn't consider that a problem. She doesn't consider it at all.

Momentarily putting to one side the disastrous population explosion that each intact male sets off, a tom leads a life of pain and hardship. Driven by his tyrannical urge, he ranges far and wide, risking his life in traffic and other assorted dangers. He is in a supercharged condition, tightly wound up and in a fever of excitement to mate (times without number) and to fight rivals whenever the need arises. The need arises constantly, and when toms fight it is a grave matter. The sound is like that of demons and banshees and the reality is worse. The result is most often bites, deep puncture wounds that tend to heal over the tops and form abscesses underneath. Besides being cruelly painful, an abscess is a massive amount

For a time, after every meal Alan
struck a Hallowe'en-cat attitude
that we came to recognize as a sign
that he had eaten a sufficiency.

of infection for such a small body to deal with. The temperature soars, and many's the cat who, untended or sometimes tended, has died of an abscess. Being what is euphemistically called "altered" adds years and contentment to a male's life.* It also causes him to turn his loving attention on his owners more than he could have done in his pristine harried state. Alan, like all our cats, has been protected and prevented from becoming one of Mother Nature's battered children.

Alan is not overly vocal. He certainly gives voice when he's very hungry at feeding time, we seem to be moving slower than the occasion warrants, and he pleads with us to look alive. In the main, however, he relies on eye contact. He finds and gazes at one of us and, depending on the context and his general demeanor, we usually know or can figure out what he wants. It is quite a subtle routine, which could easily be entirely missed by the inattentive, consisting almost solely of a sustained bright and steady gaze. He establishes and maintains eye contact until the message gets through. It gets through very well indeed. Once a day-worker said to me, "Alan shined his eyes at me and asked me to let him out."

He appears to be part Siamese. He has a Siamese face or something similar, definitely not a domestic shorthair face, Siamese hind legs, Siamese weightiness in relation to size, Siamese feet; he has domestic shorthair color, tail, eyes, and voice. That he is such a hybrid is noteworthy only because he has a sad little habit which I have read is distinctly Siamese

---

*It *must not* be done too early. A young cat needs sex hormones to reach full skeletal development. There are still some veterinarians who operate at dangerously youthful ages; so the safest rule of thumb for the cat owner is to make sure that the cat, male or female, reaches the nearest possible approach to adulthood while at the same time avoiding the siring or production of kittens. (Owners of males have traditionally, even spitefully and gleefully, shirked their responsibility, but make no mistake—If the father of the kittens belongs to you, so do some of the kittens.) This generally works out to be between eight-and-a-half and nine months for males. Females used to be considered "old enough" to be spayed when they had had their cycle once. On reflection, it is manifestly absurd to imply that the ability to reproduce proves full physical (let alone mental or emotional) maturity; it is not unusual for an unprotected female of six months, as much kitten as cat and in no way fit for motherhood, to have kittens. Choose the lesser by far of two evils: Males at least eight-and-a-half months old, and females at least once in season, should be altered even though not actually quite "old enough", because the inescapable alternative—countless doomed kittens—is so horrible as to be no alternative.

Alan employs the cat's classic graphic gesture of boundless disgust. Going through the motions of covering dung with earth, he expresses with brutal frankness his opinion of the food. With him and Gaylord, this is usually a gesture of indignant refusal. But sometimes, as here, they postpone the gesture until they've eaten, suggesting that they ate something revolting only being driven by hunger. These motions are performed forcefully and at some length.

and which is said to extend to half-breeds: He sucks on a blanket. It seems that this is a trait of Siamese cats who have been taken too young from their mothers and who often, in apparent high anxiety and agitation, even chew holes in fabric.* Alan has never appeared to be agitated, nor has he chewed anything; but occasionally, when a blanket is thrown over somebody's legs or lap, he kneads the legs or lap and, purring, sucks away energetically on the blanket. Ordinarily, purring accompanied by kneading is an expression of supreme contentment; but here it is ambiguous at best, because the whole thing distinctly has the look of a kitten nursing. Even in cheerful Alan this looks pitiful.

All cats strongly wish to preserve their dignity, and they manage to preserve it in numerous unlikely circumstances, but in Alan this wish is raised to the level of a most passionately held principle of personal sovereignty. To a considerable extent, most cats seem to resign themselves to being picked up and placed elsewhere from time to time if it is done decently. Alan simply cannot bear it. To him it is galling and degrading beyond endurance to be picked up bodily in a unilateral action and carted about, or to be thwarted in some act he has begun, simply (as it must appear to him) because he is little and we are big.

Sometimes when we enter the house, the cats are inside and, for reason of weather or the hour, we want them to stay inside. Three of our cats, attempting to slip out when the door is opened, are more or less easily blocked and without noticeable trauma. Not Alan. Alan finds it more than flesh and blood can bear to be forcibly prevented from going through the opened door, even when he doesn't really want to be outside. This means that when we're met at the door by Alan we don't have a shred of a chance to stop him. He has

---

*Practically all cats were taken too young from their mothers. Their original owners wanted to "get rid of them" and their new owners heedlessly insisted on getting tiny kittens because "they're so cute." The inevitable damage is present but obscured in domestic shorthairs. Cats have been observed to be far more emotionally stable throughout life if allowed to remain with their mothers to the age of three months.

With the coming of Alan, Gaylord (unresist-ingly) had adoption thrust upon him. He loved his new little charge, but he never wavered in his primary loyalty to Grayling.

heard us, he is ready, he is set, he is on his mark, he is psyched up, he is resolute and speedy and not to be denied.

After we realized that we had no hope of stopping him and got a glimmer of how important it all was to him, we no longer made any effort to stop him. Given this opportunity, he made himself clear to us. We come in, he shoots out, in a matter of two to five minutes we open the door, he comes straight back in. He has made his point and he's satisfied and relaxed. He's back inside and we're satisfied and relaxed. A clear case of everybody's winning and everybody's getting prizes, and nobody's composure disturbed by an undignified scuffle. It is only right to treat Alan with this respect and, both practically and humanely, it is infinitely preferable to having a resentful cat with his self-respect damaged, his nerves raw, and his disposition soured, and ourselves feeling like bullies.

After Alan had bolted out unopposed and voluntarily come right back in enough times to know that he had got his message through what he might be forgiven for thinking of as our thick human heads, he didn't any longer pop out regularly. His viewpoint had been met with acceptance and he no longer felt the erstwhile needling necessity.

The classic demonstration of Alan's entirely reasonable attitude took place as first dark neared on a raw, cold day. I had gone outdoors for some now forgotten reason, and Alan caught sight of me. He came cantering up, calling out his own small and dulcet purling greeting, and I delightedly picked him up and hugged him. We shared a warm little moment. Then it occurred to me that I might as well take him inside for the night. I had taken only the first few steps toward the house when Alan grasped my intent and began kicking and throwing himself about obstreperously. I set him down. And what did he do? He went trippingly beside me right up to the front door, and when I opened the door he serenely preceded me into the house.

In Alan's first weeks with us he was wild to make friends with all the cats, and in his youthful want of tact he

The Cats at Christmas

If there's anything that brings a cat hotfoot, it's the wrapping and tying of packages or the unwrapping and untying of packages. In the weeks before Christmas, our cats are stimulated to sprees of pryings and pokings. Never is there so much rustly paper so copiously spread about, never such reels of ribbon and metallic cord, and never so many bags and boxes.

They amuse themselves with pre-Christmas flurry as well as that of the day itself. They congregate while presents are being embellished with gaily colored boxes, paper, and bows; despite killjoy interference they unwind ribbon and cord, making festoons that rouse them to heights of frolic; they hop in and out of boxes, dear to the hearts of all cats; and they stand, companionably if not helpfully, on cartons being readied for the post office. The unwrapping of presents before the tree on Christmas morning is equally festive for them, it seems.

They are interested observers as we deck the halls—with evergreen boughs and with Georgia pine cones gathered many a long year ago—and they have a special fondness for a pine-cone wreath. Wherever this wreath has been set down before being put in place or after being taken down at the end

there. Grayling too clung close by, generally under the overhang of the built-in sofa, from which sheltered position he had a close and unimpeded view of the tree.

This was young Alan's first Christmas, but he hardly caught a glimpse of the tree. We got him two days after Christmas, with a serious and contagious-to-cats respiratory infection that demanded separate quarters. When he was convalescing and free within the house, he was so thrilled that there were other cats here that he absolutely, and automatically I believe, blanked the tree out. For him it simply wasn't there. He did take a fancy to the wreath when it was taken down from the front door, and for several days he was frequently ensconced in its inhospitable circle.

I always go with reluctant feet to dismantle a Christmas tree, partly because it's Gaylord's wondrous and much loved hidey-hole. The most recent tree was of such girth that the difficulty of getting it through the one door that would barely accommodate it didn't bear repeating; so we cut off the branches in the living room. When the once shapely tree stood stripped of light and ornament and most of each branch, Gaylord would still go padding under the meager remnants to nap. Tree and cat, considered separately or together, were pathetic.

The taking down of the tree is a time for recurrent wondering and longing to know what might be going on in those so charmingly rounded furred heads, Gaylord's in particular. When he sees the tree being destroyed, is it a doleful day for him? Does he speculate bleakly on whether or not there will ever be another? Does he figure that, as there were others before, there may be others again? Does he grieve privately for his lost treasure? When of necessity he goes back to bed, laundry box, and closet shelf, all serviceable and cozy nests but very ordinary, does he ever yearn for that bright and aromatic tree? He never openly laments but, given Gaylord's docile and unobtrusive nature, that counts for nothing. How good it would be if we could reassure him.

100

*"If men exclude any of God's creatures from
the shelter of compassion and pity, they will deal
likewise with their fellow men."*

St. Francis of Assisi

*Sometimes ascending,
debonair,
An apple tree or lofty pear,
Lodged with convenience
in the fork, . . .*
WILLIAM COWPER

Afterword

In a world where man assumed his place in nature and allowed other creatures their own rightful places, in a society that humanely prevented overpopulation of domestic animals, my husband and I would surely have had pets but not through the grisly opportunities that confronted us.

Through the years we have been accompanied by a long procession of glorious cats, two to eight abreast, every one of them plucked from circumstances which would have meant their death. Acquiring cats in this way, with never any choice, we could not possibly have done better by ourselves. This is not unusual.

Yet there is a currently popular veterinarian-writer offering in national magazines and on television advice on, among other things, how to choose and buy a cat. For him the pound and the homeless, abandoned (*Not* "stray"; *abandoned*) cat is non-existent. He recommends purchase as if there were no other way, appearing to be of the opinion that this is the only means of getting a "good" cat.

If what one wants is a pet, all cats are good cats. The need is for good owners.

If what one wants is a status symbol, that's a personal problem.

There are those who, genuinely wanting a pet for pet's sake, still cannot be satisfied except by a cat to their specifications. They have reasons, such as having had happy experiences with a certain breed or the similarity of color or pattern with some dearly loved pet of former days. I can only say, echoing Miss Jean Brodie in her prime, "For those who like that sort of thing, that is the sort of thing they like." Nonetheless, for those who have in mind something particular, the pound can, sad to say, most likely oblige them. From time to time a sizeable pound can furnish almost any kind of cat that could be called for. The reason is that countless kittens are being wrongfully born and wrongfully but inescapably suffering and dying, many in pounds. This is chiefly because so many people are not preventing their cats from reproducing, but partly because so many are already flocking to sellers to get "good" cats.

Insistence on purchase as the only proper way to acquire a pet is unrealistic and cruel and even a certain degree stupid. Most rescued cats are fundamentally healthy, and if you get a temporarily sick or frightened cat, where is the disaster? You would have saved its life, you would invest some extra time and affection in it, and you might well find yourself with a cat something like Gaylord, Grayling, Trilby, or Alan. Aside from those who have overriding preferences, personal and highly specific, anybody who could not be supersaturated with satisfaction with such a cat must be looking for something other than a pet and probably should abandon the whole idea of an animal and buy a nice pot plant. Possibly a plastic plant. It might be more satisfactory for a person who wants only a cat who is never sick, never lonely, never in need of any kind of care or consolation, in short a not-for-real animal.

Apparently it is a bitter pill for "civilized" people to swallow, the recognition that man is only a part of nature, and at that not some godlike creature having nothing in common with the rest, in splendid isolation as king of the mountain and with peculiar right to use and abuse all else at whim. As all the world knows, or as much of the world has had abundant opportunity to know, mankind's whim and practice of expediency over principle may well bring the planet to end with neither a bang nor a whimper but with the suck and suffocation of our own garbage.

Since time immemorial much of mankind has been shoring up its fragile though outsized and inflamed ego by finding people to despise. If on no other subject, these improbable allies, despisers and despised, concur on the notion of the intrinsic worthlessness of animal life. In this ugly illusion, everything from the Bible to Edna St. Vincent Millay has been cited for questionable justification and sanction. Tormented abominably as prisoners of war or as inmates of the prisons and jails that our society still tolerates, men and women habitually protest that they have been "treated like animals." Quite as if it were altogether meet and proper to perpetrate abominable cruelty on animals. "Shot down like a dog," goes the callous and vicious cliché. (Why should a dog be shot down like a lump of clay?) Men so violent that they become rapists are referred to with sickening regularity as "animals." (Ludicrous when one reflects that the human male is, with one exception, the only animal who rapes.)*

In light of man's raging brutality to his own kind, it is perhaps a forlorn hope that treatment of animals might improve. Yet historic conquest, rape, and pillage of nature are now somewhat out of favor in some circles. We have begun tardily, insufficiently, and not without acrimonious dissension, to try to slow or lessen destruction of the elements on which our lives all depend. It would be a grand thing if, as we lay claim to building a new respect for the natural environment, we did not give ourselves the lie by failing to make significant provision for wild and domestic animal welfare as

---

*It has been discovered recently that rape does occur among orangutans. Let it be remembered that the orangutan "trembles on the brink of human speech" and is not called "man of the woods" for nothing. As one of the anthropoid apes, he is zoologically very close to man. This leaves intact my point that a man who commits rape is not behaving like an animal. To the contrary. An orangutan committing rape is behaving like a man.

a matter of national policy.

There can be no rational consideration of a closer alliance with the rest of nature that excludes due assistance to animals in general. It is perhaps an all but groundless hope, but it is remotely possible that the new attention to environment could develop into a genuine principle widely embraced. Such a principle could bring us to a heightened regard and decent provision for our human poor, aged, ill, for all those of diminished powers—and for the blameless animals.

It could be the making of us.

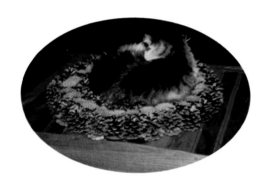